D0793989

)5ᵇ

Noah's ark in paper & card

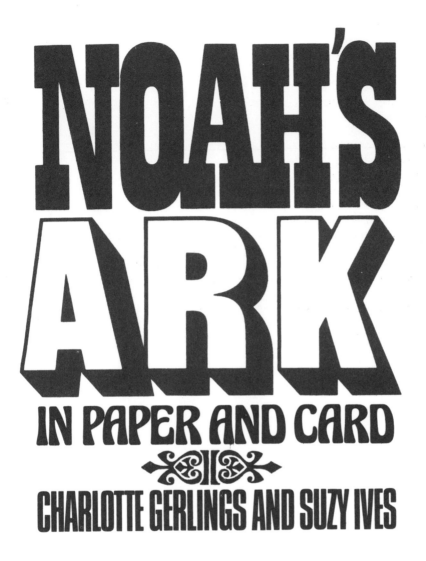

NOAH'S ARK

IN PAPER AND CARD

CHARLOTTE GERLINGS AND SUZY IVES

TAPLINGER PUBLISHING CO., INC.
NEW YORK

First published in the United States in 1974 by
TAPLINGER PUBLISHING CO., INC.
New York, New York

Library of Congress Catalog Card Number: 73-17673

ISBN 0-8008-5578-7

Contents

For Anna

Introduction

Noah's ark has traditionally been one of the basic nursery toys. Here we have attempted to produce simple patterns and instructions for making Noah, his family, the ark and forty-two different pairs of animals

The basic material is card; a cheap but strong medium that is easy to obtain and easily worked. The finished ark and animals are sufficiently robust to withstand constant handling and the animals are of a size comfortably picked up and held by small hands. The ark itself is scaled to accommodate all the figures so that they can be stored safely when not in use

The ark could be used as a classroom project for young children. It may form an aid to counting as well as to recognising and naming all the domestic animals and many of their wild kin. Since the figures are based on geometrical shapes, there is the added bonus of children becoming familiar with the construction of cubes, cones, trapezoids and other solid forms

For older children, as a craft project, the ark provides a basis for the study of animal markings, the use of colour on three-dimensional planes and practise in accurate cutting and fitting

Nimble-fingered parents can make the ark at home quite cheaply, since few tools are needed and no expensive equipment required

Materials

Scissors
A large pair with blades at least 152 mm (6 in.) long
A small pointed pair with blades about 50 mm (2 in.) long

A scalpel or craft knife
For scoring creases and trimming long straight edges

A metal straight edge
For use with the craft knife

A ruler
305 mm (12 in.) is quite adequate

Pencils
Keep very sharp. HB or B are most suitable

Rubber
A plastic rubber will clean the card without ruining the surface

Tracing paper
Choose a type that can be scribbled over without tearing. The
trace patterns are no larger than 254 mm (10 in.)

Graph paper
25 mm (1 in.) squares. A sheet 786 mm (31 in.) × 533 mm (21 in.)
will take the enlarged shape of the ark sides

Glue
We have found *Evostic* impact adhesive is the most suitable. If
applied *fairly* thickly, it will allow enough time to push the tabs
of the figures into position. It bonds extremely well and is
transparent. This glue also has a solvent for removing unwanted
blobs

Compasses
A small pair for drawing the basic shapes of the Noah family and
the circular animals

Masking tape
Used to strengthen joints of ears or paws where the card might
become worn

Colouring materials

Felt and fibre tip pens containing either water or spirit-based inks give considerable cover in a range of brilliant colours. Thick or chisel-tipped pens cover large areas of card quickly. Fine, pointed pens are ideal for detail

A suitable range of colours for the ark and animals:

Thick pens: Cadmium yellow, cadmium orange, warm grey, brilliant pink (when this is put over the orange it makes bright red) and black

Fine tipped pens: Ochre, rust, dark brown, crimson, scarlet, lemon yellow, light green, viridian, olive, light blue, dark blue, violet, magenta, flesh pink, pale grey and black (2)

Although we recommend felt pens as being reasonably colour-fast, you may use inks which give brilliant, translucent colours but tend to fade in direct sunlight

If you are making the arc and animals much larger than the trace patterns, poster or powder paints are cheaper alternatives

Staplers

A large stapler for the ark. A small stapler for the spider, turtle and Noah family

Paper clips and carbon paper are a help when transferring trace patterns to the card

Card

The ark: 5 sheets 4 ply card measuring 810 mm (32 in.) × 533 mm (21 in.)

Also two shoe boxes or small grocery boxes

The animals: 12 sheets 2 ply card measuring 810 mm (32 in.) × 533 mm (21 in.)

Choose a card with a fairly smooth surface, keep it flat not rolled

Fuse wire

15 amp. A small card will be sufficient for making the insects.

General instructions

Graph patterns
The scale of the graphs for the ark sides and both decks is one square on the graph to one 25 mm (1 in.) square on the finished ark. Draw the pattern up full size on the graph paper and cut the shape out. Use the cut out shape as a guide to the outline of the card shape

Trace patterns
These are the correct size. Trace the pattern on to stout tracing paper using a soft pencil and light pressure (if you press too hard, you will damage the book and find it hard to retrace the patterns a second time if needed). Fix the tracing paper to the page with a paperclip. This will prevent the tracing paper sliding about

A The carbon paper method: Place a sheet of carbon paper over the right side of the card, carbon side downwards. Place the tracing over the carbon paper, tracing side upwards. Secure all three sheets with paperclips. Re-draw over the traced lines using a steady and even pressure. Remove the paperclip, tracing paper and carbon paper from the card and then draw over the carbon lines on the card. (Do not press too hard either on the tracing paper or the card)

B Scribbling method: Scribble over the back of the traced paper under the tracing. Clip the scribbled tracing paper to the card, scribble side down and re-draw the traced lines. Remove the tracing paper and re-draw the pattern on the card, using the impression as a guide. Work carefully. The patterns must be transferred accurately

Colouring and cutting out

The patterns are coloured before they are cut out, this helps to prevent 'curling' of the card

Use felt pens or inks and try to colour accurately. Outline the features of the animals with a fine black line. Take the colour over the tabs and over the edges (felt pens and inks give a transparent colour and the pencil guide lines can be seen clearly through the colours)

When the colours are absolutely dry, cut out the pattern round the edge

The edge to be cut is shown by a solid black line on the trace patterns, any other lines, inside the edge of the pattern that need to be cut, are indicated with appropriate letters

Cut the patterns out carefully, even a mistake of 3 mm ($\frac{1}{8}$ in.) will make it difficult to fold the animal up into its final shape

Scoring

This is done with a craft knife. The tip of the knife is pulled gently across the card, cutting through only the surface of the card, do not score too deeply. Scoring lines are marked on the patterns by dotted lines

Folding

All folds are made away from the scored line, that is, the scoring is on the outside of the fold. When the animals are cut out and scored, it is a help if the animal is folded up into its final shape before the glue is applied, this way any slight mistakes can be checked before the final stage

11

Gluing
Place the pattern flat on a smooth surface. Apply glue to the tabs, (usually to the right side of the tabs), apply enough glue to completely cover the tab, taking the glue to both the inner and outer edges. Press the tabs to their appropriate edges in the order shown in the instructions for each animal. The final tabs can be gently slid into place

Repainting
Sometimes, when the scored lines are bent back, the scoring shows as a white line, this should be painted out

Reinforcement
Some of the animals have large ears, wings or feet which tend to get loose or worn on the folds. These edges can be reinforced with tiny strips of masking tape, these are stuck to the finished animal and then coloured over so that they are not noticeable

Mr Noah

Note: Mr and Mrs Noah, Ham, Seth and Japeth are identical in their construction. In addition to the card, you will need five ping-pong balls which should be undented, clean and free from grease, ready to be painted. You will also need a small stapler. The trace pattern given here is for Mr Noah who wears a long carpenter's apron and a cloak over a long undergarment. The style of clothing is adaptable for Mrs Noah and her sons, ideas for suitable variations are given on page 17

Transfer the trace pattern to the card. You may find it easier to use a pair of compasses at this stage, particularly if you intend to put a patterned border onto the cloak
Paint as indicated
Cut out the pattern round the edge shown by the solid line
Cut round the sleeve shapes X and Y with a craft knife
Cut slots in the arms at points XX and YY, these should be long enough to allow the sleeves to slide through without difficulty
Bend along each scored line
Bend the shapes round to form a cone, there will be a considerable overlap, giving the impression of two layers of clothing
Slide the sleeve X through slot XX and sleeve Y through slot YY
Adjust the cone shape until the double thickness is achieved and any patterned edges are level, hold together firmly and staple the shape at neck and hem line
Apply glue to the underside of each sleeve
Stick down over the arms of the figure, the sleeves should come to wrist length
Bend the feet up

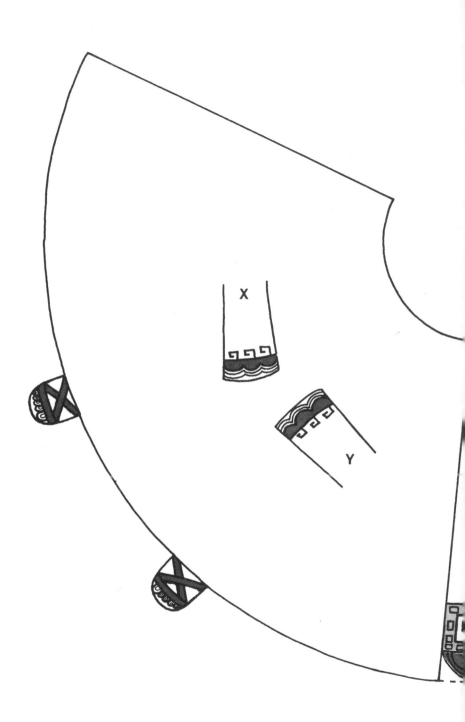

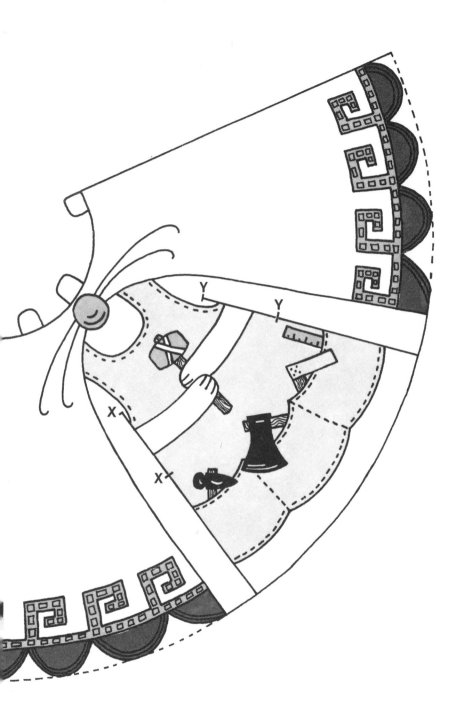

The heads

Acrylic (plastic) paints or model aircraft enamels in tiny paint tins are most suitable for applying to the ping-pong balls, suggested patterns for faces are shown

When the paint is dry, apply glue to the tabs at the neck of the cone and press the ping-pong ball head down onto them so that it fits firmly

A little pressure from your hand *inside* the cone will help

Mrs Noah, Ham, Seth and Japeth

The ark

Sides

Transfer the pattern from the graph to a large sheet of card, use the first side, when cut out and coloured, as a template for the second side. The second side must be the other way round so place the completed first side *face down* onto the second sheet of card and draw round it. The colouring then follows a similar pattern. Staple the front and back edges of the two halves of the ark together, about 6 to 12 mm ($\frac{1}{4}$ to $\frac{1}{2}$ in.) from the edge. Staple at 12 mm ($\frac{1}{2}$ in.) intervals. Cut the ramp edges where shown

Waves

Transfer the waves pattern to the card in the same way, not forgetting to reverse the second side, paint them and staple them together at the front and back edges as before. The waves fit round the base of the ark

Foundation

This is a box for the lower deck to rest upon so that the ramp, when open, leads straight in to the doors of the lower house. The box measures 252 mm (10 in.) long by 177 mm (7 in.) wide by 138 mm ($5\frac{1}{2}$ in.) high. Cut down an old shoe box to get these measurements. The box is positioned in relation to the ramp-opening, as centrally as possible. Glue the long sides of the box to the inside of the ark

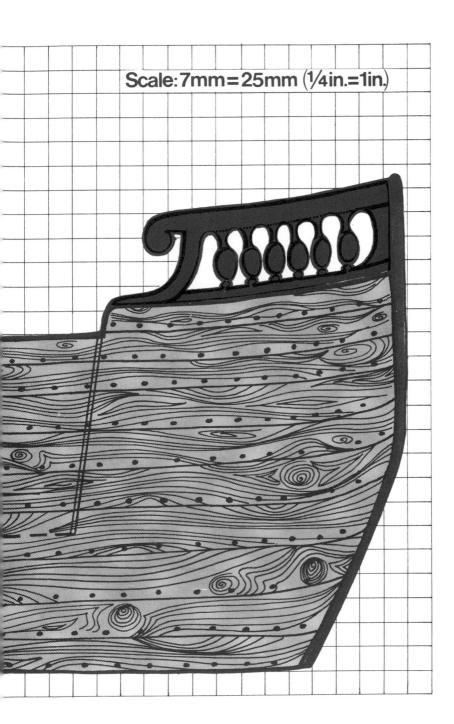

Scale: 7mm=25mm (¼in.=1in.)

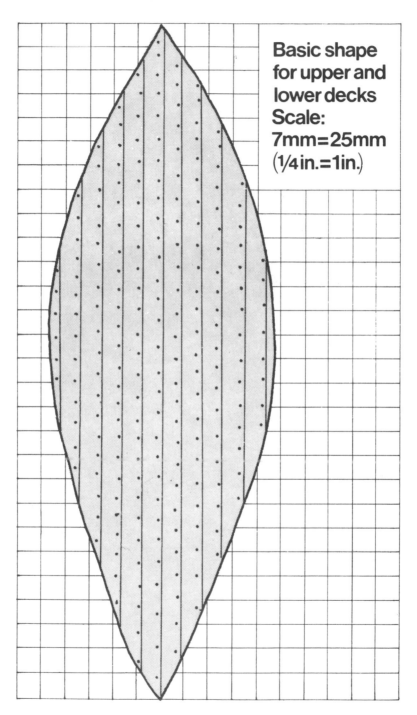

**Basic shape
for upper and
lower decks
Scale:
7mm=25mm
(¼in.=1in.)**

22

Lower house

The lower deck
Transfer the lower deck shape to the card from the graph pattern.
Trim to fit where necessary. Colour the lower deck so that it
resembles planks nailed together. Apply glue to the top of the
foundation box and press the lower deck into position

The lower house
This is made from a normal-sized shoe box. If the shoe box is of
plain card, simply colour it. If it is already coloured, cover the
original colour with white paint and then colour over the paint.
Throw the lid away and using the box upside-down, cut door
edges as shown in the diagram. Place the finished lower
house onto the lower deck

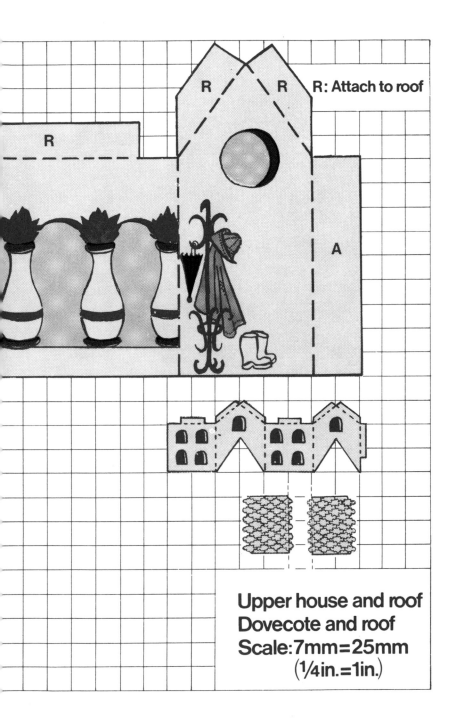

R: Attach to roof

**Upper house and roof
Dovecote and roof
Scale:7mm=25mm
(¼in.=1in.)**

The upper deck

This is made in exactly the same way as the lower deck, trimmed to fit where necessary and stuck into position on top of the lower house. Colour the front edge of the upper deck to match the flat surface

The upper house

Transfer the scaled pattern onto a large sheet of card. Colour in the details

Suggested colours:

Walls: plain white or pale grey

Doorway and windows: red edges, turquoise background

Bead curtain: multicoloured

Pillars: yellow with blue and red stripes, red base

Acanthus leaves at top of pillars: green, blue and red

Hat stand: brown

Sou'wester and rain cape: yellow

Umbrella: orange and white

Gumboots: grey with yellow welts

Sacks: beige and white

Barrels: light brown, dark brown with grey hoops

Bay tree: green

Bottle: brown

Potted herbs: green in light brown pots

Jug: turquoise

Corn: yellow

Onions: beige and green

Cut out round the edges shown by solid lines and score on the right side where indicated by the dotted lines. Bend the house round into a box shape and glue the tab A to the inside of the back wall. Bend the tabs (marked R) inwards to hold the roof

26

The roof

Transfer the scaled pattern onto a piece of light card. Draw in the tile pattern keeping it as even as possible. The roof may be coloured red all over or in a combination of four or five related colours. Suggested colours: purple, magenta, light pink, orange-brown and beige. Cut out the shape round the edges paying special attention to the tile edges. Score on the right side down the centre of the roof where indicated by the dotted line and fold in half. Apply glue to the tabs marked R on the house shape and stick the roof to these. Be sure to get an even overhang at each gable end. Pressure from your hand *inside* the house shape will help. The upper house stands on the upper deck as shown in the drawing

The dovecoat

House section: Transfer the scaled pattern onto a piece of light card. Leave the walls white and colour the window edges red with black background. Cut out the pattern round the edges indicated by the solid line. The angle of the cut which fits the apex of the upper house roof should be 65 degrees. Score on the right side where indicated by the dotted lines. Bend the dovecote round into a box shape and follow the instructions given for the *upper house* tab arrangement

Roof section: Transfer the scaled pattern onto a piece of light card. Draw in the tile pattern keeping it as even as possible. The roof may be coloured blue-grey all over or in a combination of four or five related colours. Suggested colours: purple, grey, light blue, light green and olive. Cut out the two halves round the edges paying special attention to the tile edges. Score each half on the *wrong* side where indicated by the dotted lines. Fold these edges upwards and glue them back to back to form a small ridge down the centre of the roof. Apply glue to the tabs on the house section and stick the roof to these, following the instructions given for the *upper house*

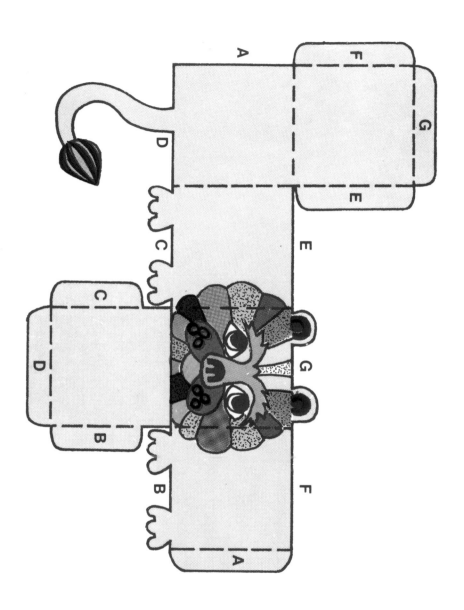

Lion, tiger and leopard

Transfer the trace pattern to the card
Paint as indicated
Cut out the pattern round the edge shown by the solid line
Score the pattern on the right side where indicated by the dotted lines
Bend along each scored line
Apply glue to the right side of the tabs
Stick the tabs down in alphabetical order
Bend the tail up and repaint any scored lines if necessary.

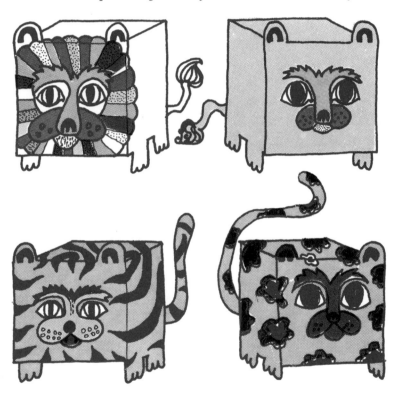

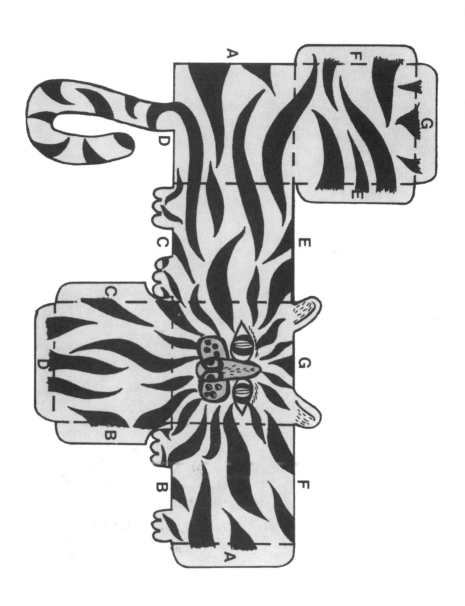

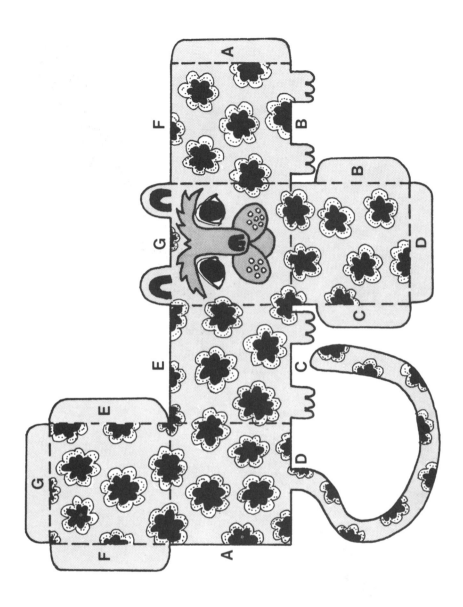

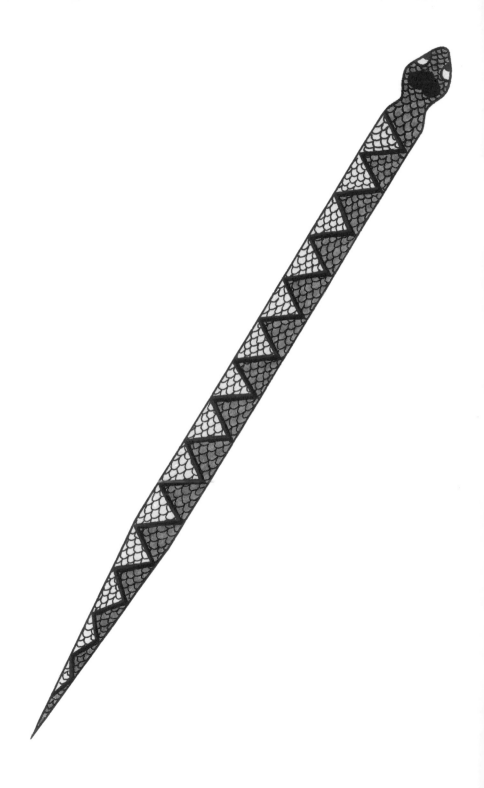

Snake

Transfer the trace pattern to the card
Paint as indicated
Cut out the pattern round the edge shown by the solid line
Turn the shape over and paint the underside in a single bright colour
Curl the shape into a spiral round a pencil.

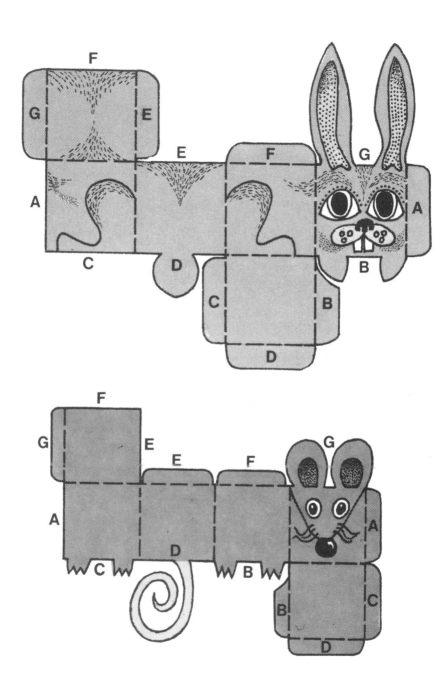

Rabbit and mouse

Transfer the trace pattern to the card
Paint the right side as indicated
Cut out the pattern round the edge shown by the solid line
Paint the underside of the ears and tail on both the rabbit and
mouse, and the underside of the paws on the rabbit
Score on the right side where indicated by the dotted lines
Bend along each scored line
Apply glue to the right side of the tabs
Stick the tabs down in alphabetical order
Rabbit: bend the tail up and the paws forward
Mouse: bend the tail up
Repaint any scored lines if necessary.

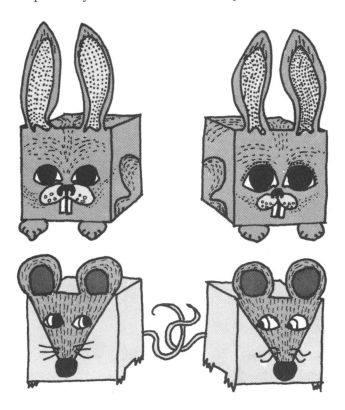

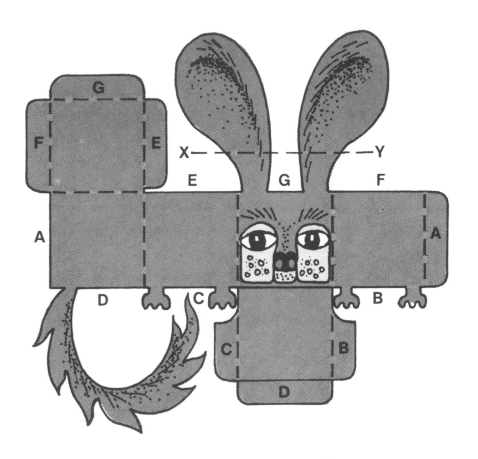

Dog

Transfer the trace pattern to the card
Paint the right side as indicated
Cut out the pattern round the edge shown by the solid line
Score the pattern on the right side where indicated by the dotted line
Bend along each scored line
Apply glue to the right side of the tabs
Stick the tabs down in alphabetical order
Bend the ears forward at line XY
Repaint any scored lines if necessary, paint the underside of the ears pink.

Owl

Transfer the trace pattern to the card
Paint the right side as indicated
Cut out the pattern round the edge shown by the solid line
Paint the underside of the wings, feet and tail
Score on the right side where indicated by the dotted lines
Bend along each scored line
Apply the glue to the right side of the tabs
Stick the tabs down in alphabetical order
Bend the tail and feet up
Repaint any scored lines if necessary.

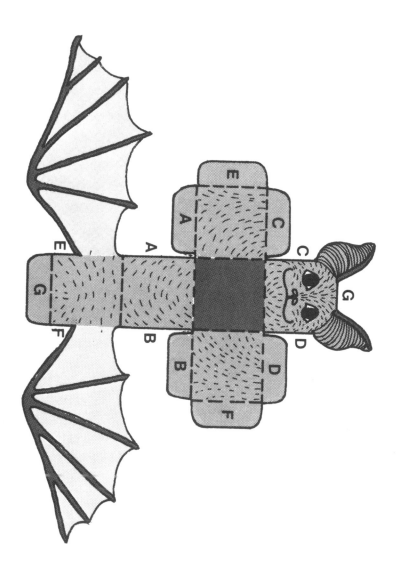

Bat

Transfer the trace pattern to the card
Paint the right side as indicated
Cut out the pattern round the edge shown by the solid line
Paint the underside of the wings and the back of the ears
Score on the right side where indicated by the dotted lines
Bend along each scored line
Apply glue to the right side of the tabs
Stick the tabs down in alphabetical order
Repaint any scored lines if necessary.

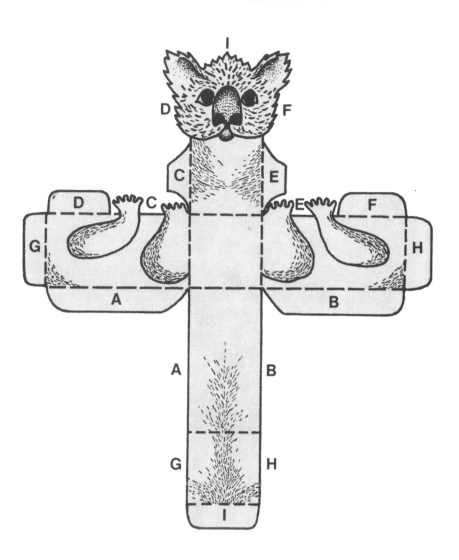

Koala

Transfer the trace pattern to the card
Paint the right side as indicated
Cut out the pattern round the edge shown by the solid line
Turn the shape over and paint the back of the ears and paws
Score the pattern on the right side where indicated by the dotted lines
Bend along each scored line
Apply glue to the right side of the tabs
Stick the tabs down in alphabetical order
Repaint the scored lines if necessary.

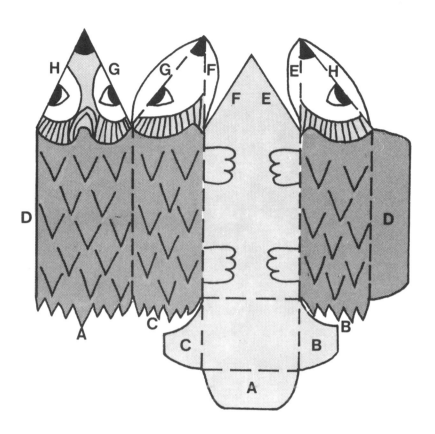

Hedgehog

Transfer the trace pattern to the card
Paint the right side as indicated
Cut out the pattern round the edges shown by the solid line
Score on the right side where indicated by the dotted lines
Using a sharp craft knife, carefully cut round the shape of the
feet (indicated by the solid lines) and cut the v-shapes for the
spines (also indicated by the solid lines)
Push the feet out from the wrong side and bend them up at right
angles
Do the same with the spines
Bend along each scored line
Apply glue to the right side of the tabs
Stick the tabs down in alphabetical order
Repaint any scored lines if necessary.

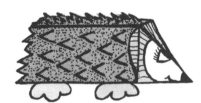

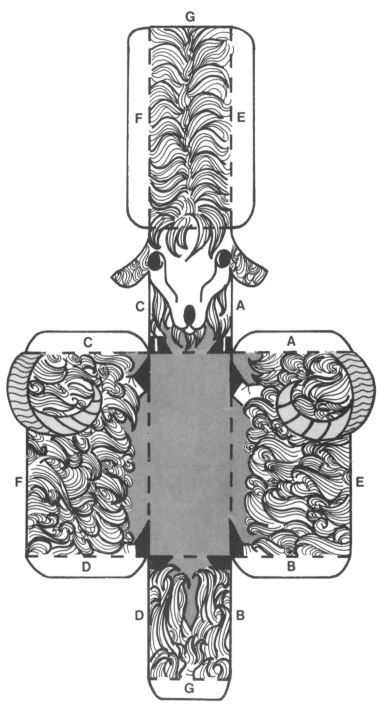

Ram and sheep

Transfer the trace patterns to the card
Paint the right side as indicated and draw in the curly coat
Cut out the pattern round the edge where shown by the solid line
Paint the back of the ears and (ram) the back of the horns
Score the pattern on the right side where indicated by the dotted lines
Bend along each scored line
Apply glue to the right side of the tabs
Stick the tabs down in alphabetical order
Repaint any scored lines if necessary.

Butterfly

Transfer the trace pattern to the card

Paint the right side as indicated

Cut out the pattern round the edge shown by the solid line

Turn the shape over and paint the other side to match the right side

Score the pattern on the underside where indicated by the dotted line

Bend along the scored line

Take a 127 mm (5 in.) length of 15 amp fuse wire, tie a loose 'knot' in one end of the wire

Using a fine needle, make a hole where indicated on the pattern

Thread the unknotted end of the wire through the hole, pull the wire down until the 'knot' rests against the butterfly, bring the wire up, over the front of the butterfly and back through the loop of the 'knot' and the hole

Pull the wire down again so that the butterfly is firmly held.

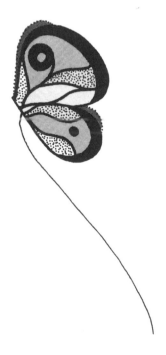

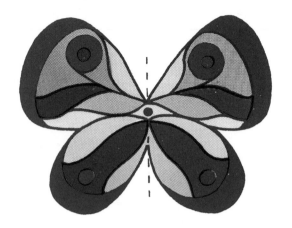

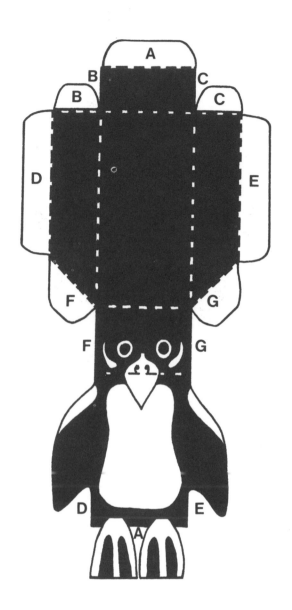

Penguin

Transfer the trace pattern to the card
Paint the right side as indicated
Cut out the pattern round the edge shown by the solid line
Turn the shape over and paint the back of the wings and the underside of the feet
Score the pattern on the right side where indicated by the dotted lines
Bend along each scored line
Apply glue to the right side of the tabs
Stick the tabs down in alphabetical order
Bend the feet forward and repaint any scored lines if necessary.

Chimpanzee

Transfer the trace pattern to the card
Paint the right side as indicated
Cut out the pattern round the edge shown by the solid line
Turn the shape over and paint the back of the arms and tail
Score the pattern on the right side where indicated by the dotted lines
Bend along each scored line
Apply glue to the right side of the tabs
Stick the tabs down in alphabetical order
Bend the tail up and the arms down
Repaint any scored lines if necessary.

Cat

Transfer the trace pattern to the card
Paint the right side as indicated
Cut out the pattern round the edge shown by the solid line
Turn the shape over and paint the back of the ears and tail
Score the pattern on the right side where indicated by the dotted lines
Apply the glue to the right side of the tabs
Stick the tabs down in alphabetical order
Bend the tail up
Repaint any scored lines if necessary.

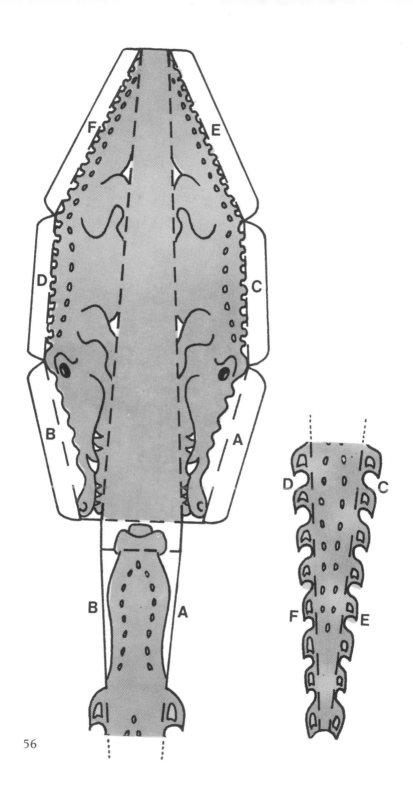

Crocodile

Transfer the trace pattern to the card
Paint the right side as indicated
Cut out the pattern round the edge shown by the solid line
Turn the shape over and paint the underside of the back section
Score the pattern on the right side where indicated by the dotted lines
Apply glue to the right side of the tabs
Stick the tabs down in alphabetical order
Bend up the spines along the back at right angles
Repaint any scored lines if necessary.

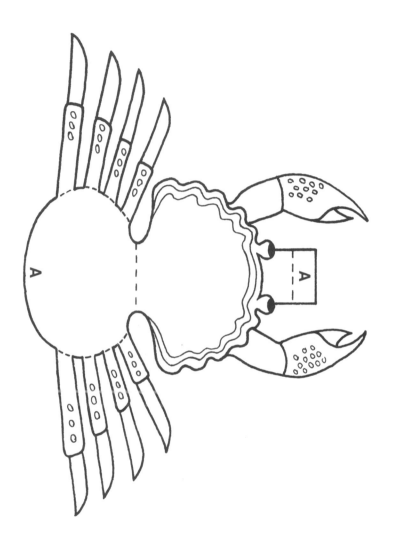

Crab

Transfer the trace pattern to the card. The leg features are drawn on the *other* side of the shape and should be simply outlined at this stage
Paint the right side as indicated
Cut out the pattern round the edge shown by the solid line
Take care to make clean cuts round the eyes without cutting off the gluing tab
Turn the shape over and mark in the leg features
Paint the underside as indicated
Score the pattern on the right side of the shell and gluing tab where indicated by the dotted line; also along the line between the eyes and where the legs join the body
Turn the shape over and score the leg joints as indicated by the dotted lines
Bend along each scored line
Apply glue to the tip of tab A (right side) and press tab A to the edge of the body section at point A
Repaint any scored lines if necessary.

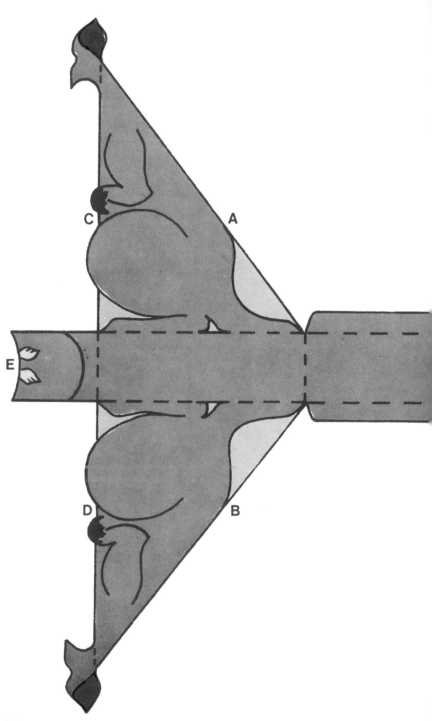

60

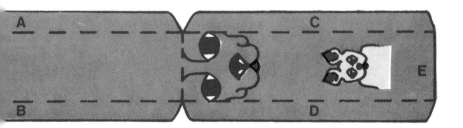

A

C

B

D

E

61

Kangaroo

Transfer the trace pattern to the card

Paint the right side as indicated

Cut out the pattern round the edge indicated by the solid line

Turn the shape over and paint the back of the ears and the inside of the knees and paws

Score the pattern on the right side where indicated by the dotted lines

Turn the shape over and score just below the ears where indicated

Bend along each scored line

Apply glue to the right side of the tabs

Stick the tabs down in alphabetical order

Apply glue to the inside of the upper face, fold the upper face and ear sections round so that they stick to the front of the main structure

Repaint any scored lines where necessary.

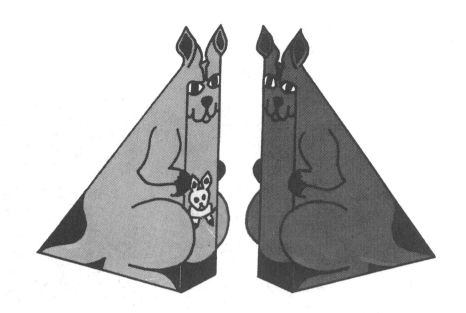

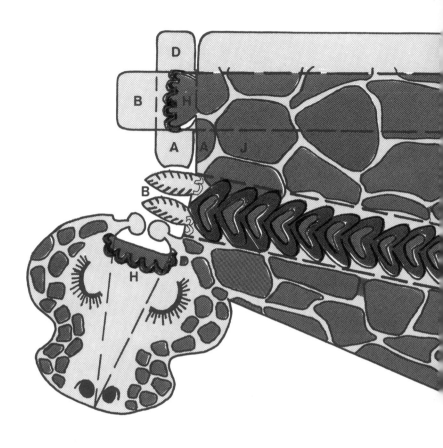

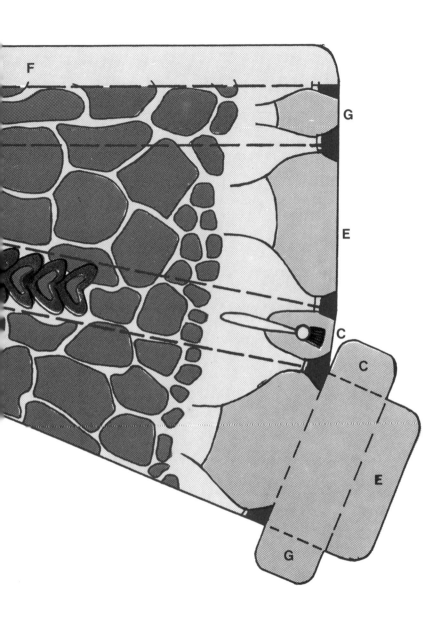

Giraffe

Transfer the trace pattern to the card
Paint the right side as indicated
Cut out the pattern round the edge indicated by the solid line
Turn the shape over and paint the back of the ears and horns
Score the pattern on the right side where indicated by the dotted lines
Bend along each scored line
Apply glue to the right side of the tabs and to the *underside* of each cheek
Stick the tabs down in alphabetical order
The free side of the head (cheek section) is stuck to the upper neck at J
Repaint any scored lines where necessary.

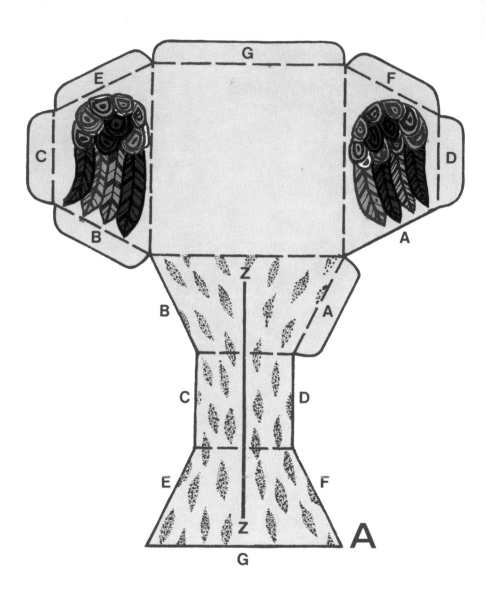

G

E   F

C   D

B   A

B   Z   A

C   D

E   F

Z

G   **A**

B

C

69

Cock and hen

Transfer all three shapes (A, B and C) from the trace patterns to
the card, *repeat shape* A since this is the body section common to
both cockerel and hen
Paint the right side as indicated
(Suggested colours for the cock: blues and greens. Suggested
colours for the hen: browns and pinks)
Cut out the patterns round the edges shown by the solid lines
Turn shapes B and C over and paint to match the right side
Score both shapes A on the right side where indicated by the
dotted line
Cut a slot between z and z on each shape A with a craft knife
Bend along each scored line
Apply glue to the right sides of the tabs on each shape A
Stick the tabs down in alphabetical order
Repaint any scored lines if necessary
Push the base of the cockerel shape C into the slot zz on cockerel
shape A
Push the base of the hen shape B into the slot zz on hen shape A.

Duck

Transfer all three shapes (A, B and C) from the trace patterns to the card
Paint shape A solid yellow
Paint shapes B and C as indicated
(Suggested colours for the drake: blues, greens and purples.
Suggested colours for the duck: browns and greys)

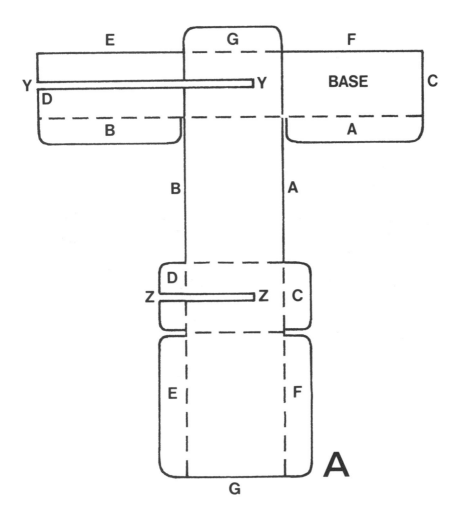

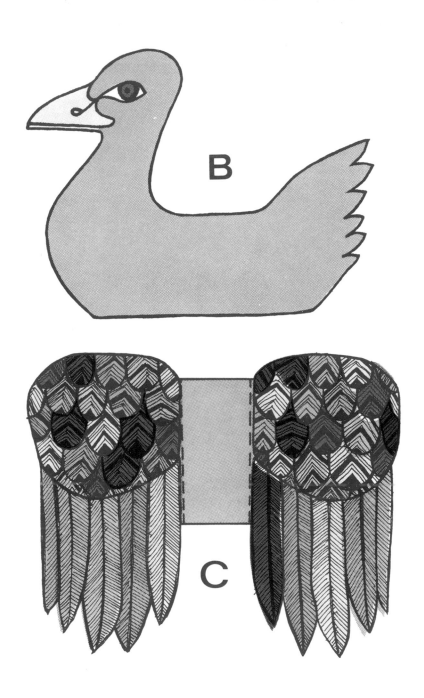

B

C

Cut out the patterns round the edges shown by the solid lines
Turn shape B over and paint the other side to match
Turn shape C over and paint the underside solid yellow
Score shape A on the right side where indicated by the dotted lines
Cut slots along the lines YY and ZZ on shape A with a craft knife
Bend along each scored line
Apply glue to the right side of the tabs on shape A and the underside of the central panel between the wings on shape C
Stick the tabs down on shape A in alphabetical order
Glue the underside of the central section of shape C to the base of shape A
Glue the underside of the wings and bend them up and press them into contact with the sides of shape A
Push the base of shape B into the slot YYZZ on shape A
Repaint any scored lines if necessary.

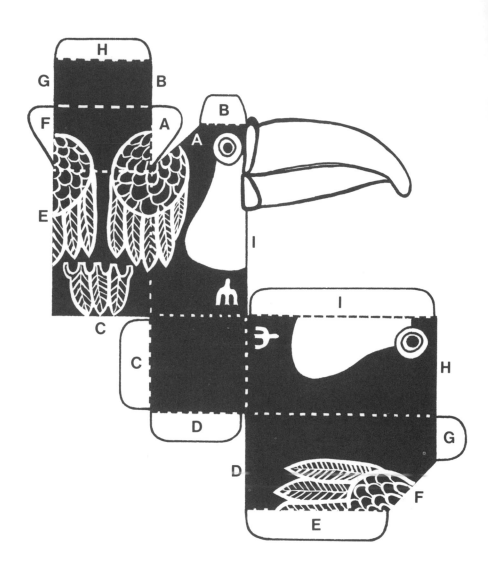

Toucan

Transfer the trace pattern to the card
Paint the right side as indicated
Cut out the pattern round the edges shown by the solid line
Turn the shape over and paint the other side of the beak
Score the pattern on the right side where indicated by the dotted lines
Bend along each scored line
Apply glue to the right side of the tabs
Stick the tabs down in alphabetical order
Repaint any scored lines if necessary.

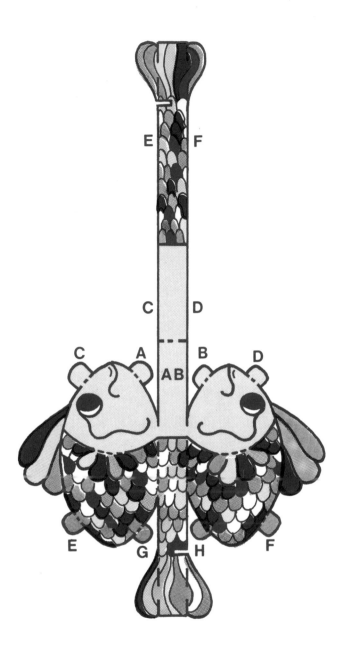

Fish

Transfer the trace pattern to the card
Paint the right side as indicated
Cut out the pattern round the edge shown by the solid line
Turn the shape over and paint the underside of both tail sections
to match the right side
Score the pattern on the right side where indicated by the dotted
line and cut round the fins with a craft knife
Cut two slots just below the tail fins
Cut these slots to exactly *half* the width of the tail
Bend along each scored line
Apply glue to the right side of the tabs
Stick the tabs down in alphabetical order and slot the two tail
sections together so that they fit flush
Paint the back of the fins and repaint any scored lines if
necessary
Note: The fish is not designed to be free standing, it should be
tucked between the hull of the Ark and the frieze of waves.

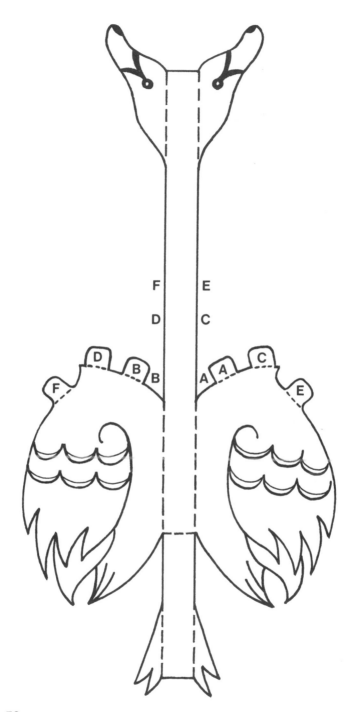

Swan

Transfer the trace pattern to the card
The head features are drawn on the *other* side of the shape and should be simply outlined at this stage
Draw in the wing and tail feathers as indicated
Cut out the pattern round the edge shown by the solid line
Turn the shape over and draw in the head features
Paint the beak as indicated
Score the pattern on the right side of the tail and body where indicated by the dotted lines
Turn the shape over and score along the head where indicated
Bend along each scored line
Apply glue to the right side of the tabs and to the underside of each beak section
Stick the tabs down in alphabetical order, the beak sections are stuck together at the tip
Bend the neck round a pencil to give it an s shape
Note: The swan is not designed to be free standing, it should be tucked between the hull of the ark and the frieze of waves.

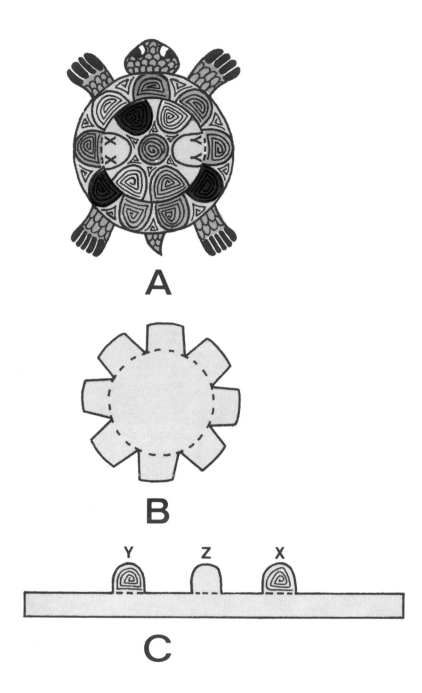

A

B

Y   Z   X

C

Turtle

Transfer all three shapes (A, B and C) on the trace pattern, to the card

You will find it easier to use a pair of compasses than to trace freehand

Paint the right sides as indicated

Cut out each shape round the edge as shown by the solid lines, taking care to make clean cuts round the tiny tabs

Turn shape A over, paint the underside of the head, tail and legs to match the right side and paint the rest of the underside green

Score on the right sides of shapes A, B and C where indicated by the dotted lines

Cut slots at XX and YY on shape A

Bend along each scored line

Take shape B and using a *small* stapler, staple each pair of adjacent tabs until you have produced a pill-box shape, with the tabs bent up to form the sides

Apply glue along the length of the wrong side of shape C

Bend shape C round shape B to conceal the staples

Take the body section (formed by shapes B and C) and with tabs X and Y pointing upwards, insert them through the slots on shape A (tab X through slot XX and tab Y through slot YY)

Apply glue to the underside of tabs X and Y and press them down so that they match the decoration on shape A

Apply glue to the underside of the head and press tab Z firmly into position.

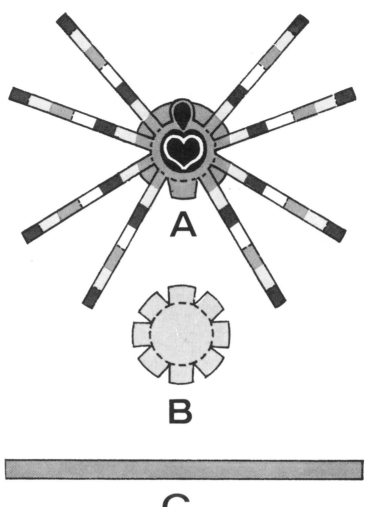

A

B

C

Spider

Transfer all three shapes (A, B and C) from the trace patterns to
the card
You will find it easier to use a pair of compasses than to trace
freehand
Paint the right sides as indicated
Cut out each shape round the edge as shown by the solid lines,
taking care to make clean cuts round the tiny tabs
Turn shape A over, paint the underside in a single bright colour
Score on the right sides of shapes A and B where indicated by the
dotted lines
Turn shape A over and score on the legs where indicated
Bend along each scored line
Take shape B and using a *small* stapler, staple each pair of
adjacent tabs until you have produced a pill-box shape, with the
tabs bent up to form the sides
Apply glue to the right side of the tabs on shape A
With these tabs pointing downwards, insert them into the newly
constructed shape B, pressing gently until the two sections fit
firmly together
Apply glue along the length of shape C (wrong side)
Bend shape C round the body of the spider to conceal the staples
Repaint any scored lines if necessary.

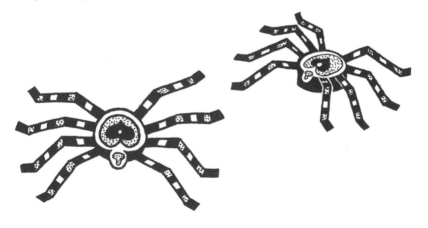

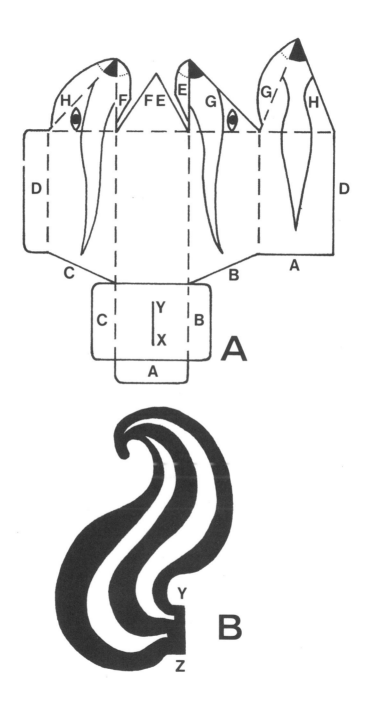

Skunk

Transfer both shapes A and B from the trace patterns to the card
Paint the right side as indicated
Cut out the patterns round the edges shown by the solid lines
Turn shape B over and paint the other side to match
Score shape A on the right side where indicated by the dotted lines
Cut slots in shape A between XX and YY with a sharp craft knife
Bend along each scored line
Apply glue to the right side of the tabs on shape A
Stick the tabs on shape A down in alphabetical order
Push the base of shape B (YZ) into the slot on shape A
Repaint any scored lines if necessary.

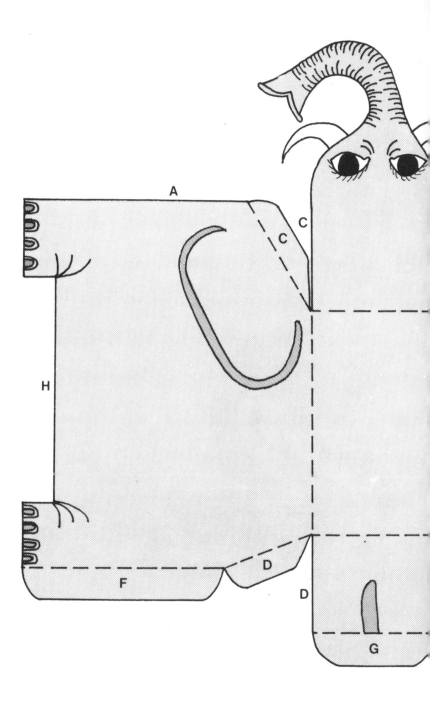

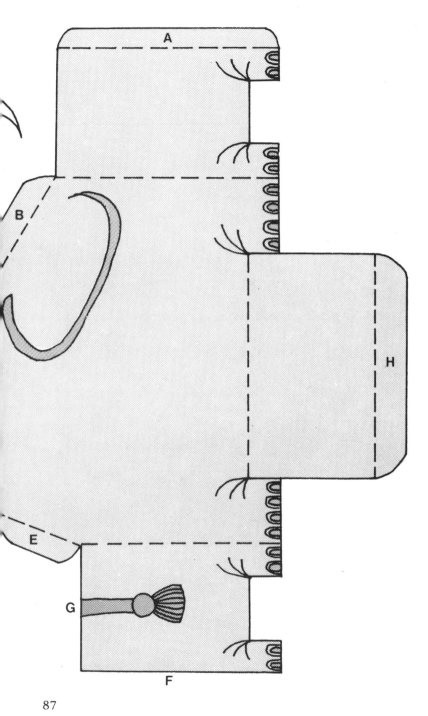

Elephant

Transfer the trace pattern to the card
Paint the right side as indicated
Cut out the pattern round the edge as shown by the solid line
Score the pattern on the right side where indicated by the dotted lines
Bend along each scored line
Apply glue to the right side of the tabs
Stick down the tabs in alphabetical order
Stick down the little triangular flap that joins the two halves of the right front leg, bend the tusks up
Repaint any scored lines if necessary.

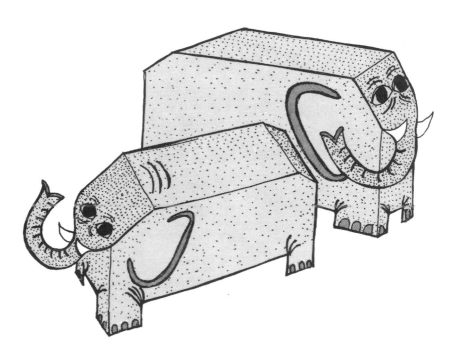

Hippopotamus and pig

Transfer the trace pattern to the card
Paint the right side as indicated
Cut out the pattern round the edge as shown by the solid line
Score the pattern on the right side where indicated by the dotted line
Bend along each scored line
Apply glue to the right side of the tabs and to the underside of the face section
Stick the tabs down in alphabetical order
Tab E folds up under tabs F and G and the face section is pressed down firmly into contact with all three
Repaint any scored lines if necessary
An alternative face section for the pig is shown beside the trace pattern for the hippopotamus.

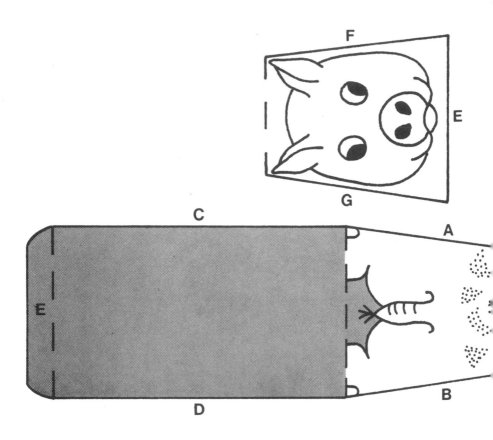

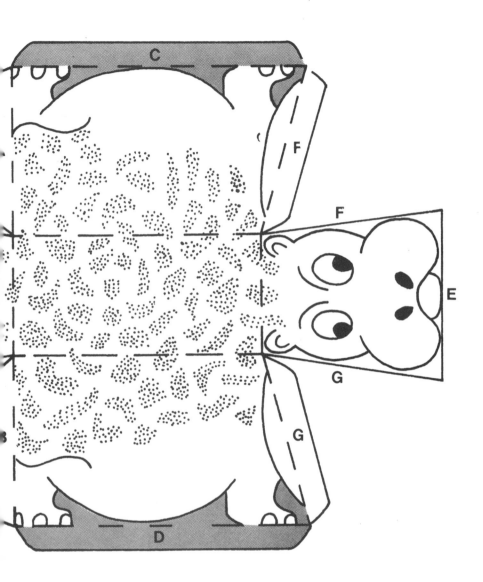

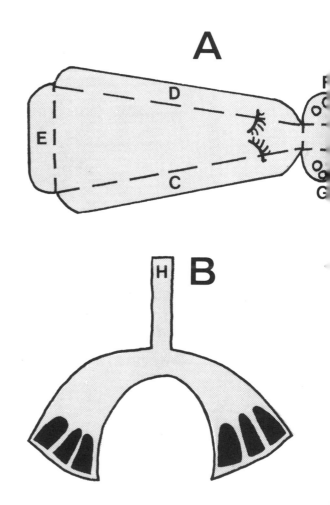

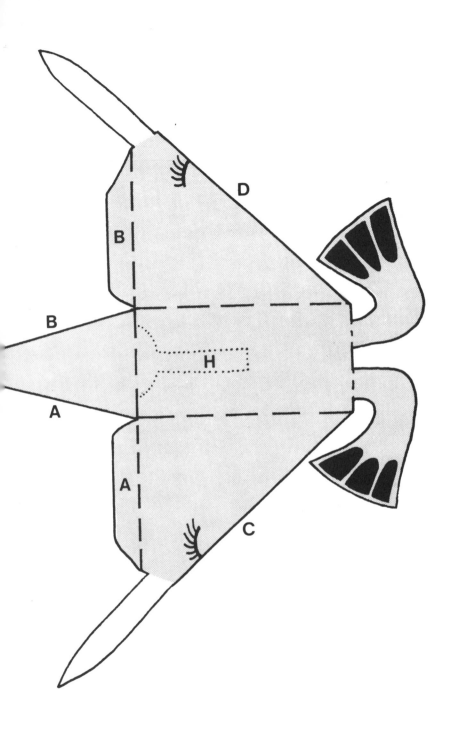

Walrus

Transfer both shapes (A and B) from the trace patterns to the card
Paint the right sides as indicated
Cut out the patterns round the edges indicated by the solid lines
Score shape A on the right side as indicated by the dotted lines
Bend along each scored line
Apply glue to the right side of tabs A, B, C, D and E and to the
underside of tabs F and G
Stick the tabs down in alphabetical order, tabs F and G are
pressed into contact with either side of the muzzle
Glue the right side of tab H and stick this to the underside of the
body at point H as marked
Repaint any scored lines if necessary.

Ladybird and bee

Transfer the trace pattern to the card
Paint the right side as indicated
Cut out the pattern round the edge shown by the solid line
Turn the pattern over and paint the underside black
Using a fine needle, make a hole where indicated
Take a 254 mm (10 in.) length of 15 amp fuse wire and thread one
end of the wire through the hole in the ladybird or bee so that a
short length shows on the other side
Bend the short length of wire round and pinch it flat against the
card so that the ladybird or bee is held firmly
Make another ladybird or bee and attach it to the other end of
the wire in the same way.

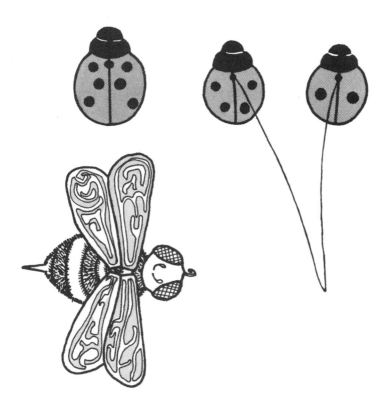

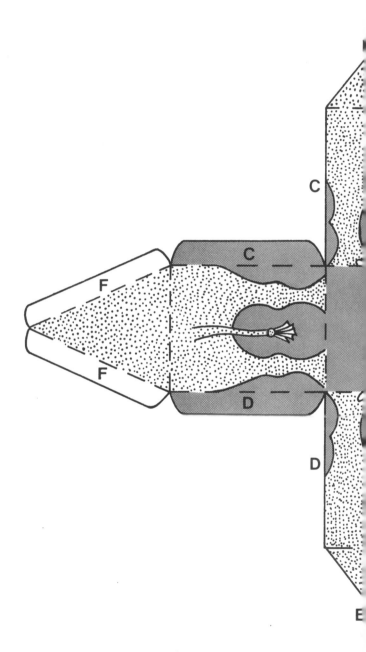

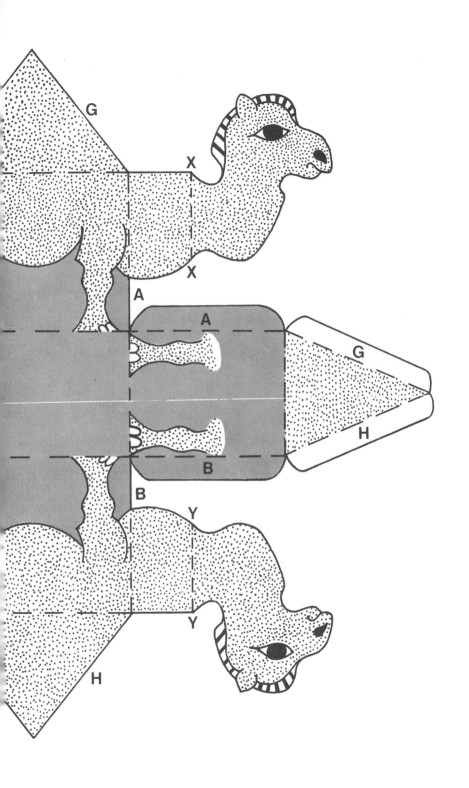

Camel

Transfer the trace pattern to the card
Paint the right side as indicated
Cut out the pattern round the edge shown by the solid line
Score on the right side where indicated by the dotted lines
Turn the shape over and score along lines xx and yy on the neck
Bend along each scored line
Apply glue to the right side of the tabs
Stick the tabs down in alphabetical order, the two side hump
sections are pressed firmly into contact with the last four tabs
to form a pyramid
Apply glue to the back of the two head and neck sections
Fold these sections so that the base of the neck is stuck to the
front of the main structure
The rest of the head and neck sections are stuck to one another
Repaint any scored lines if necessary.

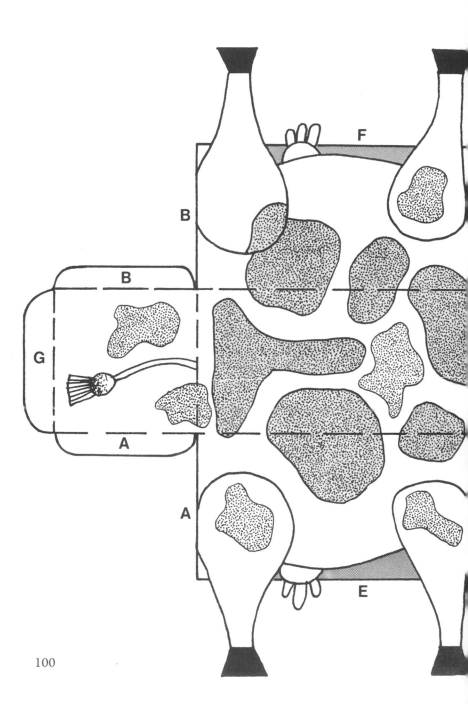

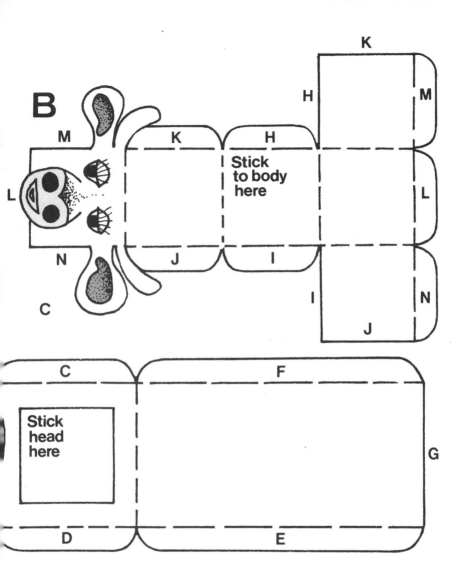

B

K

H

M

M

K H

Stick to body here

L

N

J I

L

I

N

J

C

A

C F

Stick head here

G

D E

D

Cow and bull

Transfer both shapes (A and B) from the trace patterns to the card
Paint the right sides as indicated
Cut out the patterns round the edges shown by the solid lines
Turn the patterns over and paint the underside of the legs, ears and horns
Score on the right sides where indicated by the dotted lines
Bend along each scored line
Apply glue to the right side of the tabs
Stick the tabs down in alphabetical order
Apply glue to the back of the head section and stick the head to the front of the body where indicated
Repaint any scored lines if necessary
Adapt the bull from the cow pattern by omitting the udders, making the face fiercer and the horns more pointed.

Locust

Transfer the trace pattern to the card
Paint the right side as indicated
Cut out the pattern round the edge shown by the solid line
Turn the shape over and paint the underside pale brown
Score on the right side where indicated by the dotted line
Fold *firmly* along the scored line and stand the locust upright.

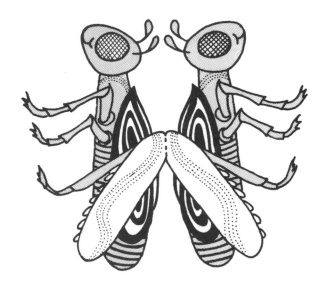

G

F

D

C

104

E

F

G

D

C

B

A

A

B

Zebra, horse and reindeer

Zebra

Transfer the trace pattern to the card
Paint the right side as indicated
Cut round the pattern as indicated by the solid line
Turn the shape over and paint the other side of the ears
Score the pattern on the right side where indicated by the broken line
Bend along each scored line
Stick the tabs down in alphabetical order
Apply glue to the free side of the head (cheek section) and stick to the upper neck at H
Press the sides of the nose down gently
Repaint any scored lines where necessary

Horse
Transfer the outline to the card as for the zebra
Omit the stripes and draw in long hair on the mane and tail
Follow the rest of the instructions as before

Reindeer
Transfer the outline to the card as for the zebra
Instead of tracing the ears, follow the pattern for the antlers
indicated by the dotted line
Omit the zebra's stripes and mane and draw in the tail without
a tuft on the end
Follow the rest of the instructions as before.

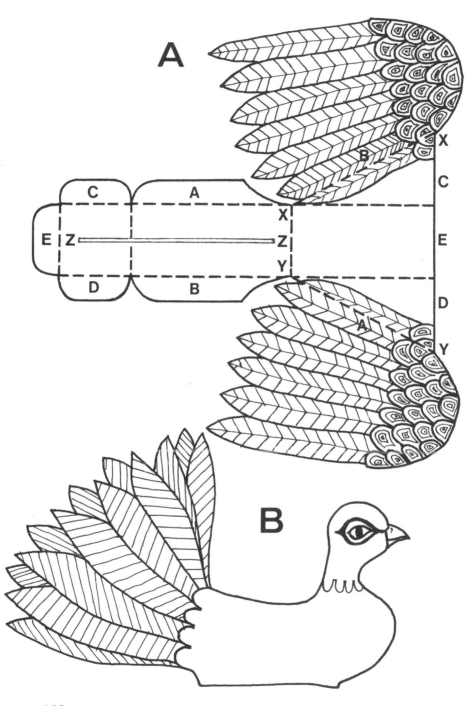

Dove

Transfer both shapes (A and B) from the trace patterns to the card
Draw in the feathers on shape A as indicated; and on shape B,
draw in the feathers and head features, then paint the head a
delicate pink and the beak a bright red
Cut out the patterns round the edges shown by the solid lines
Turn shape A over and draw in the feathers on the underside of
the wings
Turn shape B over and draw in the feathers and head features,
then paint the head and beak to match
Score shape A on the right side where indicated by the dotted
lines
Turn shape A over and score along lines XX and YY
Cut a slot between Z and Z on shape A with a sharp craft knife
Bend along each scored line
Apply the glue to shape A on the right side of the tabs
Stick the tabs down in alphabetical order
Push the base of shape B into the slot ZZ on shape A
Bend the wings downwards.

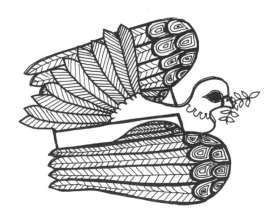

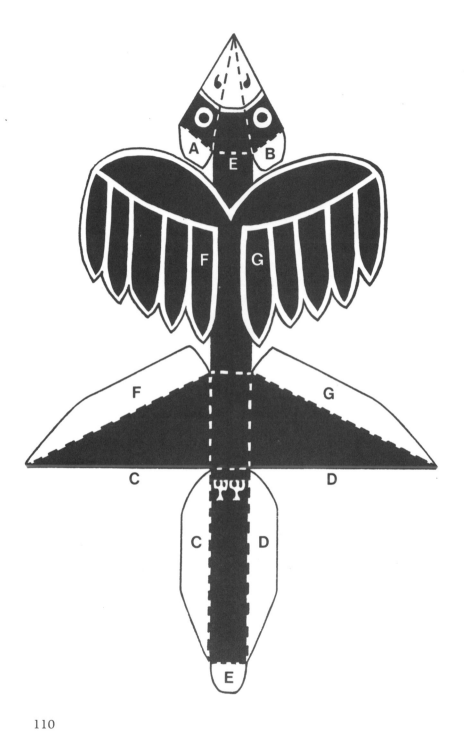

Raven

Transfer the trace pattern to the card
Paint the right side as indicated
cut out the pattern round the edge shown by the solid line
Turn the pattern over and paint the underside of the wings and head black
Mark in the feathers on the underside wing in white
Score the pattern on the right side where indicated by the dotted lines
Bend along each scored line
Apply glue to right side of tabs A and B, bend these tabs round so that the glued sides of A and B come into contact with the underside of the neck. To do this it will help if the sides of the beak/head are bent into their final positions, see illustration
Now glue all the other tabs on the right side and stick them down in alphabetical order: this will form the triangular body shape
Tab E is slipped under tabs F and G (which overlap) and the whole body is then brought up with the point at E slipping into the pocket formed by the head
Note: Although this sounds complicated, practise the assembly first as this will make final assembly easier
Repaint any scored lines if necessary.

Suppliers

Great Britain

Card, paper, paints and inks
Fred Aldous, The Handicrafts Centre
37 Lever Street, Manchester 760 1UX
E.J.Arnold (School Suppliers)
Butterley Street, Leeds LS10 1AX
Crafts Unlimited
Macklin Street, London WC2
Dryad Ltd, Northgates, Leicester
Educational Supply Association
Pinnacles, Harlow, Essex
Margros Ltd
Monument Way West, Woking, Surrey
Clifford Milburn Ltd
54 Fleet Street, London EC4
Nottingham Handcraft Company
(School Suppliers)
Melton Road, Westbridgford
Nottingham
(Not paints or inks)
Reeves and Sons Ltd, Lincoln Road
Enfield, Middlesex
George Rowney and Company Ltd
10 Percy Street, London W1
Winsor and Newton Ltd, Wealdstone
Harrow, Middlesex
also local art suppliers

Felt-tip pens
Speedry Products Ltd
Copers Cope Road, Beckenham, Kent
(Broad felt markers,
Studio Colour range)
(Schwan-Stabilo fine fibre-tip pens, Series 68)
and local art suppliers

Glue
Evostic Impact adhesive
from stationers and general stores
Local art suppliers and stationers
will provide the following:
Tracing paper, graph paper, masking
tape, craft knives and compasses

USA

Card, paper, paints and inks
Arthur Brown and Bros Inc
2 West 46 Street
New York NY 10036
The Craftool Company
1 Industrial Road, Wood-Ridge,
New Jersey 07075
A.I.Friedman Inc
25 West 45 Street
New York NY 10036
Grumbacher
460 West 34 Street, New York
The Morilla Company Inc
43 21st Street
Long Island City, New York and
2866 West 7 Street, Los Angeles
California
New Masters Art Division:
California Products Corporation
169 Waverley Street
Cambridge, Massachusetts
Stafford-Reeves Inc
626 Greenwich Street
New York NY 10014
Winsor and Newton Inc
555 Winsor Drive
Secausus, New Jersey 07094
And local art supply stores

Felt-tip pens
Magic Marker Corporation
88 and 73 Avenue Glendale, NY
Nobema Products Corporation
91 Broadway, Jersey City,
New Jersey
Geliot Whitman Limited
Herschell Road, London SE23 1EQ
Schwan-Stabilo
also local art supply stores